W9-BFI-229

LITTLE PANDA

THE WORLD WELCOMES

HUA MEI

AT THE SAN DIEGO ZOO

JOANNE RYDER

ALADDIN PAPERBACKS

NEW YORK   LONDON   TORONTO   SYDNEY   SINGAPORE

For everyone who loves Hua Mei and wants giant pandas to survive—
especially Jessica, Heather, and Victoria, Cory and Lee, Lucy and Molly

ACKNOWLEDGMENTS

The author is especially grateful to the Research, Animal Care, and Marketing staff at the World-Famous San Diego Zoo for their insight, graciousness, and care in the preparation and review of this manuscript, and thanks them for their kind and thoughtful assistance.

Also, I deeply thank my editor, Jessica Schulte—who first saw the need to tell Hua Mei's story—for her boundless enthusiasm, skill with words, and gentle understanding of the plights of authors and pandas.

The Zoological Society of San Diego would like to acknowledge the support of the following organizations: Zoological Society of San Diego trustees and staff, U.S. Department of the Interior, Consulate General of the People's Republic of China, State Forestry Administration, China Wildlife Conservation Association, Sichuan Forestry Department, China Research and Conservation Center for the Giant Panda, Wolong Nature Reserve, Pacific Bell and the SBC Global Network, as well as all those who continue to support the conservation and research efforts helping to save this critically endangered species.

First Aladdin Paperbacks edition March 2004

Text copyright © 2001 by Joanne Ryder
Illustrations copyright © 1999, 2000 by the Zoological Society of San Diego

ALADDIN PAPERBACKS
An imprint of Simon & Schuster Children's Publishing Division
1230 Avenue of the Americas
New York, NY 10020

All rights reserved, including the right of reproduction in whole or in part in any form.

Also available in a Simon & Schuster Books for Young Readers hardcover edition.
Designed by Heather Wood
The text of this book was set in Meta Book.

Manufactured in China
4 6 8 10 9 7 5 3
ISBN 0-689-84310-0 (hc) / LC# 00-111905
A minimum of 5% hardcover and 4% paperback of the net retail proceeds will go to worldwide giant panda conservation efforts of the World-Famous San Diego Zoo.
Hua Mei and World-Famous San Diego Zoo® are trademarks of the Zoological Society of San Diego. Used with permission.
For more information about giant pandas, please contact
Pacific Bell Giant Panda Research Center
San Diego Zoo
P.O. Box 551
San Diego, CA 92112-0551
Or visit the Web site at www.SanDiegoZoo.org
ISBN 0-689-86616-X (pbk.)

A baby panda
curls within
a tender paw...
held close to her
mama's beating heart.

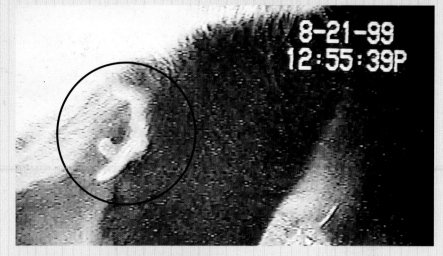

8-21-99
12:55:39P

8-21-99
12:55:12P

For the first weeks of her life, this tiny baby (circled in above photo) was viewed only with a camera in the panda den at the World-Famous San Diego Zoo. Even when scientists couldn't see the baby, who was born on August 21, 1999, they could hear her! Baby pandas can call very loudly if they are uncomfortable, frightened, or hungry.

8-27-99 FRI A00

Pink and pale,
sprinkled with white fuzz,
a tiny cub
is just a promise
of a bear to be.

9-09-99 THU A00
6:46:58A 02 C1 TL

9-09-99 THU A00
6:49:57A 02 C1 TL

9-09-99 THU A00
6:50:44A 02 C1 TL

Panda cubs are born smaller and more vulnerable than brown or polar bear cubs. At birth, a baby panda is more than 800 times smaller than her mother! The baby is cared for by her mother alone; panda fathers do not help raise cubs.

But soon
patches of dark skin
reveal the giant panda hidden within.

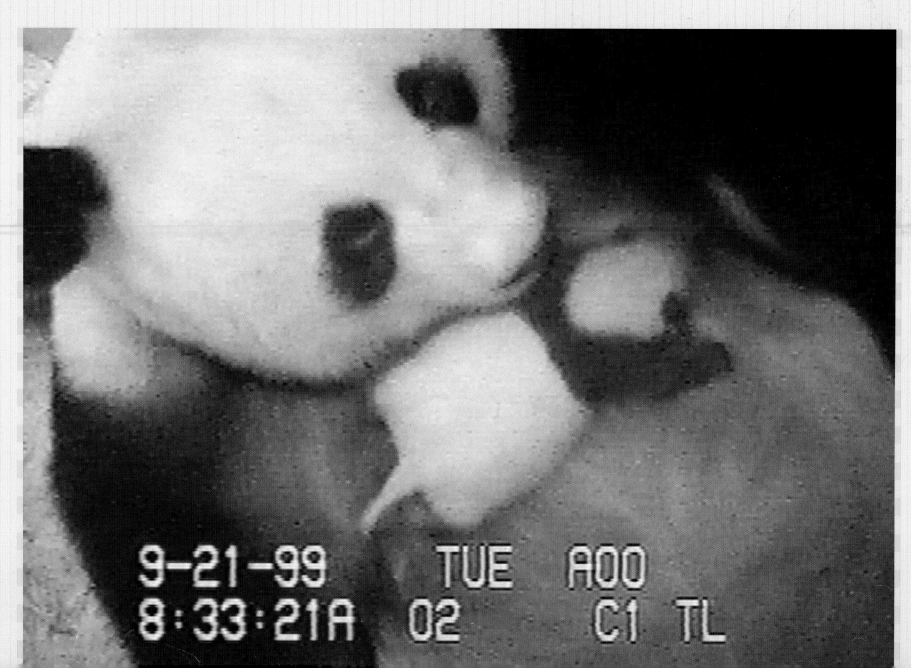

Unable to walk,
unable to see yet,
a fragile baby
gets a checkup.

Gentle people examine her,
weigh her, and measure her,
making sure she is healthy.

As she grows, they learn more about her and about all pandas.

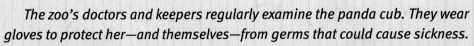

The zoo's doctors and keepers regularly examine the panda cub. They wear gloves to protect her—and themselves—from germs that could cause sickness.

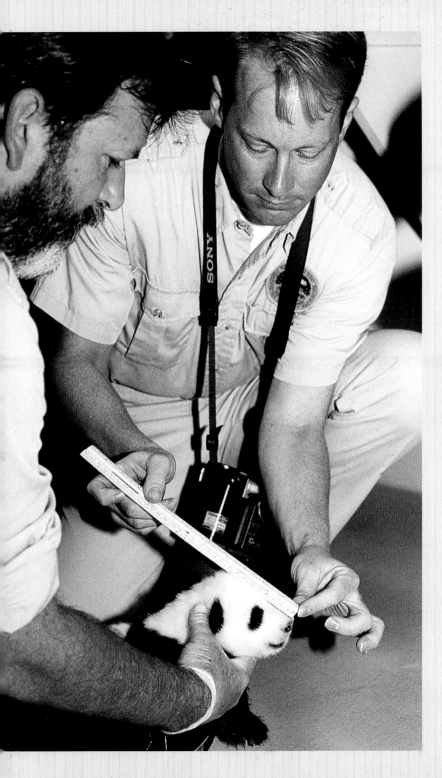

A baby panda is learning, too.
At first she can't hold up her head.
Then...

Look at her!
She is sitting
and standing now,
eager to take
her first steps.

*Pandas are born blind.
A baby's eyes open at around
fifty to sixty days, but it may
take even longer before a baby
panda can see clearly. It can
take up to four months before a
panda will take its first steps.*

One hundred days after her birth,
a little panda receives her Chinese name—
Hua Mei (pronounced *Hwa May*).

This baby connects China,
a land where pandas roam misty mountains,
to the United States, the land of her birth.

Hua Mei means "China-USA." Chinese names can have more than one meaning. Hua Mei also means "splendid beauty."

Slowly, shyly,
Hua Mei steps
into a new place,
ready to meet
and greet
the world.

Full of wonders, her new home tempts a curious panda to explore the soft grass, the tall trees.

When Hua Mei was five months old, she went outside for the very first time. Soon after, visitors were able to see Hua Mei in the zoo's Pacific Bell Giant Panda Research Station exhibit area.

There she goes—
climbing with wobbly legs,
up and up and up and up.

*Pandas are natural climbers. They use their
stronger front legs to pull themselves as they climb.*

Whoops!
She flips
upside down.

Whee!
She sits
rightside up.

A little panda finds treasure everywhere.
Just the right size, a stick becomes a toy
Hua Mei bites, tastes, and juggles in her paws.

Keepers and scientists scatter items for the pandas to discover: sometimes a burlap bag, sometimes a mound of sawdust to roll in, and sometimes a "bamboosicle"—a hollow bamboo reed filled with tasty treats to snack on.

A tiny acrobat scrambles
in her very own playground.

Hua Mei pulls and climbs,
testing the branches,
testing her own strength.

*Hua Mei loves to have her head and back gently scratched. (Her fur feels much like a German shepherd's.)
If she comes when the keepers call her, Hua Mei is rewarded with lots of scratching! Keepers need to
be able to depend on Hua Mei coming when called so that checkups and doctor visits are easy for everyone.*

Hua Mei wanders,
drawn to the
sparkling pool,
patting the water,
dipping into coolness.

A young panda
makes her own discoveries
while her mama, Bai Yun
(pronounced *By Yoon*),
feasts on bamboo.

Observers are specially trained people who take notes
about the things pandas do all day. When the pandas are
active—eating and climbing and playing—the observers
are very busy writing about what the animals do.

Pandas are known as bamboo bears because they eat up to forty pounds of bamboo a day. Their diet changes with the seasons. Sometimes they eat only the leaves and other times they chew on just the thick, woody stems.

Bai Yun grasps bamboo with nimble paws.
With her strong teeth, she crushes stems,
ripping and stripping slender leaves.

Soon Hua Mei will have all her teeth.
Then she will be a bamboo bear like her mama,
big enough to eat the tall, tall grass.

But for now, when she's hungry,
Hua Mei cuddles close to her mama,
nursing, sipping warm, rich milk.

Hua Mei
looks up
a leafy tower.
Wishing
herself high,
she starts
to climb.

Little pandas have sharp claws to help them climb trees. A mother panda doesn't worry when her baby climbs up high. Pandas are safer in the branches of a tree than on the ground where they can be hurt by other animals.

She peeks through branches
at the world below,
at her mama never very far away.

Hua Mei
tags her mama—
catch me if you can—
and runs away.

Bai Yun weighs about 200 pounds. She knows she must be gentle when she plays with little Hua Mei, who weighs only about 20 pounds in these photos.

Playful pandas roll and tumble
making up a game all their own.

Chirping softly, she feels
her mama's big arms
scooping her up,
wrapping around her,
catching her
with a hug.

One year old, Hua Mei
is a promise come true—
a lively, healthy giant panda.

Hua Mei will stay with her mother for about 18 months and then will live by herself. In nature, giant pandas live alone. They come together only to mate. Fewer than 1,000 giant pandas survive in the world today. It is important to protect these rare animals from extinction.

May she
and all pandas
live long,
be well, be safe
on our good earth.